Distant Fires

Distant Fires

poems
Doug Ramspeck

GRAYSON BOOKS
West Hartford, CT
www.GraysonBooks.com

Distant Fires
copyright © 2020 by Doug Ramspeck
published by Grayson Books
West Hartford, Connecticut

ISBN: 978-1-7335567-7-4
Library of Congress Control Number: 2019953197

Book & cover design by Cindy Stewart
Cover art by Virginia Dehn

For Beth and Lee

Acknowledgments

Alaska Quarterly Review: "Small Nation" and "User Manual"

Mid-American Review: "Sacred Departures"

Southern Review: "Shell Casings"

Contents

The Dead I Know   13

RIVER AND TRAINS

Small Nation   17
User Manual   18
Field Song   19
Shell Casings   20
Sacred Departures   22
Winter Mud   23
Temporary Self-Portrait   24
Distant Fire   26
Essay on Family   27
On the Roof   29
Rust of Rain   31
The Gift   33
From Some Other World   34
Riptide   37
Into the Curvature of Earth   39
Flashing   40

LETTERS FROM PRISON

I   45
II   46
III   47
IV   49
V   50
VI   51
VII   54
VIII   56
IX   57
X   58
XI   59
XII   61

DREAM PLAY

Act One   66
Act Two   70
Act Three   73

EPILOGUE
Coyote Moon 81
Breath 82
Winter Auguries 83

About the Author 85

The Dead I Know

I see them, sometimes, as though at a bus window,
their faces shy with death, reticent with eternity.
Maybe they are older than in life, the hair more gray,
but more often they are indeterminate in dusty glass,
as though they are that distant point where land and sky
join, where the one is almost but not quite the other.
Usually, in this vision, an ash of snow falls from a scrim
of sky. And always I lift a hand to wave, and the faces turn
to watch me recede at the road's verge, and the expressions
are a somber map, a geography of unstirred waters.
They do not wave in return. They simply stare.
And I keep my hand in the air till they are gone.

River and Trains

Small Nation

The first time my brother and I played chicken
on the railroad tracks, we leapt from the bridge

before the train was anywhere near us.
We splashed down at the same moment,

then treaded water while listening to the train
drowning out the sounds of the cicadas.

Afterwards, we lay on our backs in the current
and watched the eye of the moon rolling back

into the skull of the clouds, and we listened
to the breezes sifting through the dreadlocks

of the willows. And that winter there was often
a live wire of blue light at dusk in the field

behind our father's barn, and we studied how it lived
inside itself, how it seemed older than the moon,

its own small nation. And once we carried saucers
onto the garage roof and sledded off the edge into open

air, down into a snowdrift, and that was the same winter
my brother broke his collarbone twice, and we stole

a hunting knife and a hatchet from the unlocked shed
of a neighbor. Later, when my brother went to prison,

I would tell myself that something was already
forming on those days and nights of our childhood,

was already formed, even though we leapt
with equal abandon toward the river.

User Manual

Our mother used to say prayers
for our father's temper, as though

it were a thing living separate from
the man, some volatile creature

that might be tamed with soft words
or clasped hands. And my brother

and I would imagine those prayers
rising up the chimney then bouncing off

the clouds. And God, with one ear tilted,
would hear the words like so many bees

humming in a hive. Meanwhile, on land,
down where prayers seemed—at least

to my brother and to me—like birds
breaking their necks on window glass,

we learned a prayer of watching
closely for the sudden twitching

of our father's hands. And when,
years later, he was dying of emphysema,

I sat with him on the back porch
and watched follicles of pale light sifting

through the obelisks of corn stalks,
and studied the living funnels of dust

forming on the road as our father
gasped for air, the claws of his hands

furious in his lap.

Field Song

One winter my brother and I found a blue jay trapped beneath
the ice of the river. And when we swept away the snow

with our mittened palms, the creature looked up at us with
such anguish that we could not turn away. I was just eight

and my brother at the tail end of nine, and we watched
the afternoon light falling at a diagonal across the fence

near our father's barn. We were just off the school bus
and reluctant to head inside, so we sat on the hard ice

and spoke in sympathetic voices to the bird, which had
the dignity to say nothing back. And that night I rose from bed

while my brother slept, and stood at the window gazing
at the formalin of moon. And I imagined that the jay might peck

its way free of the ice, and fly away. And as snow fell
the next day into the field behind the house, I kept telling

my brother that I wanted to go back, wanted to search again
for the bird, and finally we walked in a gray anguish of light

to the river. Later, when I was older, I would wonder if
the winter sun as it looked down knew to love a field

no differently than it loved the water, or did its love shift
with the seasons and the weather? And I pretended that falling

snow was a love letter to the land. On this day, though, my brother
and I found the bird where it was waiting, and sang to it.

Shell Casings

I will arise and go now... —W. B. Yeats

My brother would line up the bullets
on the back porch and arrange them
in such an exact formation that I was
almost sad when he pushed the first one
into the chamber and I watched
the .22 casing fly, watched the tin can
jump or the blue jay become a confetti
of feathers or the squirrel drop
from its high limb to convulse
on the grass before growing still.
But when my brother shot Ralph,
the neighbor's cat, and we buried him
near my mother's tomato plants,
I kept remembering as we dropped his limp
body into the hole how he would rub
against my legs each time I crossed
into the next yard to ask Mrs. Orlen
if she needed her lawn cut or her weeds
plucked or her driveway shoveled.
For days we heard Mrs. Orlen
alternately calling *Ralph Ralph*
then *Kitty Baby Kitty Baby*, which
I found myself remembering last summer
when my own cat was dying slowly
of kidney failure. In Spike's final weeks,
I carried him sometimes out the back door
so we could lie together by the pond,
and I would look up at the old world
of the sky while he studied a dragonfly
flitting atop the quiet green waters.
Or I would run a hand across his fur
and recite—as best I could—the lines
from "The Lake Isle of Innisfree,"
which he seemed to appreciate,
more or less, and I spoke the words again
on the afternoon we buried him not far
from my wife's tomato plants. And as I
gripped the shovel, I remembered

how those casings would be warm
to the touch after having flown toward me
on the porch, and how Spike's fur collected
and hoarded the heat of the sun as he lay
with his eyes closed. And I recalled
my long dead brother touching a hand
to my shoulder as we stood above the grave,
and how he told me to go inside, to let him
finish up, that it was all okay, that everything
was okay, to trust him…it was okay.

Sacred Departures

Like that, my mother used to say about a neighbor
or relative who died. *Like that*, snapping her fingers.

Then later my brother and I would sit beneath
the deformed fingers of the sky, beneath the dandelion

deadheads of clouds, and snap our own fingers with
the same rhythm, speak the same words, and laugh.

But when our mother died at thirty-two—
like that, like that—I dreamed of the undulant swaying

of the years, how they arc out and out without
ever coming back, the hours broken vessels,

the decades an occultation. Once, at nine, my brother cut
his foot on a river rock then bled red into the shallows.

Here, it seemed, was the covenant of going and going
and being gone. And now that he is long dead, too,

I imagine the moon tonight as like a pale cyst above the roof.
Once, I know, my brother and I watched our father stealing tools

from the garage of a neighbor widower who had died.
Carrying them away before his family could arrive

from California. And once my brother was stung
on the eyelid by a yellow jacket. But the moon, tonight,

seems a lonely digression above the land, and while my wife
sleeps, the sky blooms a perfect black blossom.

Winter Mud

Mornings we woke sometimes to gunfire from the woods,
and stood at the bedroom window while our father

came walking across the snow with a deer on his back,
the four legs wrapped around his neck, two in each hand.

This was after our mother was gone, and my brother
punched me on the arm as we studied how the carapace

of snow made a small geography of white beneath
our father's boots, the crunching sounds a kind of dream.

Other days we came down the stairs to find dead squirrels
piled on the kitchen counter, the bushy tails tossed on

the floor. And once we saw a black snake in the sink,
a bloodied knife beside it, and our father scolded us

that he'd been up for hours, that he had no patience
for idlers or jokers. But mostly I remember the winter mud

on his jeans each time he came walking from the woods,
the morning light gathering amid the trees, the dark birds

small handkerchiefs in the sky. And from inside
the house where we were watching, the cold world

seemed framed in mute glass, the first faint flares
of day falling across the deer's lolling neck.

Temporary Self-Portrait

The houses my brother and I broke into
when we were in junior high were mostly
along the shores of Lake Elizabeth, usually
summer cabins of the wealthy, always
in winter. We stood at the windows
of these homes and watched the way
the snow unfastened itself from the clouds
then dropped to be swallowed in the gray.
And we thought of how the corridors
of our lungs drew in air then released it
back into the world, and yet, as near
as we could tell, was unchanged by the passage,
in the same way that these houses—
other than a broken window or two,
other than the liquor bottles we drank from
then shattered in the driveways,
other than the obscene designs we drew
sometimes on the walls—were unaltered
by us and cared nothing for our lives.
Sometimes I wondered how someone
could own a home then abandon it
for most of the year, could arrive there only
in bright summer light when the waters
dreamed themselves into such a devotion of blue.
But mostly my brother and I smoked cigarettes
or weed then lay on the couches or the beds,
imagining that this was our life now,
far from the strictures and fists of our father.
And sometimes I dreamed that the stars
above these roofs beneath which we were hidden
were distant flames in a far-off black woods,
that the moon was the collective belief
that only what was temporary was real. And once
I was pissing in the open maw of a toilet
when my brother began shouting that a car
had just pulled into the driveway, and out we ran
through the back door, down into the thicket
of trees that backed up to the railroad tracks.

And as we ran I glanced back to that house
as though to see my true family there, this life
that existed only as a kind of annihilation,
while my breaths and my brother's made
desperate wraiths in the winter air.

Distant Fire

When my brother first obtained his driver's license
and was able to borrow our father's truck, we drove
some nights to the quarry, sneaked through a hole
in the fence, and drank beer and dropped rocks
into what seemed such a perfect black void
that we imagined that the sound of the splash
was tearing into the fabric of the world.
Often, though, on the ride back, he would stop
at his girlfriend's house and knock on her bedroom
window, while I sat lonely in the car or sometimes
in the back lawn, on lookout in case lights came on
from the bedroom of the parents. One night,
I remember, I sat with a beer in my lap while the first
snow of the season came drifting from the sky,
and in the darkness it seemed more gray than white,
like the ash of some distant and invisible fire.
I kept thinking about what my brother was surely
up to inside that darkened window, and to me it seemed
as mysterious as that stone dropping into what often
appeared far below us like the blown pupil
of an eye. But when at last my brother emerged
over the windowsill and we went strolling back
to the car, and I asked for him to tell me what it was like,
he shrugged and said it wasn't like anything at all,
which I took, at the time, as something profound,
but which I now believe was him telling me to shut up.

Essay on Family

Some families, of course, appear fine,
just fine, but who can really know for sure

whether, in private, they make some art
of quarreling, some biting into the green

sourness of words? I woke most mornings
to hear the voices of my father and brother

rising and trembling though the floorboards,
their arguments existing, always, in the same

narrow space, performing ever-smaller
migrations, concentric circles disappearing

in a bowl. *Get off my back*, my brother said.
Get a job, my dad said. Or *Get better friends*.

And of course there were warnings all around us:
the cataracts of clouds at night and the pelvis

curve of moon, the days skinning themselves
into open cysts, my brother hiding a handgun

beneath his shirt some nights when he drove us
into town. But now I imagine those hours

floating past in a kind of formalin, the years
something we rolled in our fingers then cracked

like walnuts, the trapdoor of decades appearing
like the liquid iris of an eye. And on the night

he pressed the barrel of that pistol to my neck,
we had been drinking on the porch and studying

how the lacuna of snow slept in the backyard
beneath an albino moon, and the sepulchral

fields beyond the fence were a pale pale.
That he didn't pull the trigger was the first

miracle of the night, and the second was later
when our father joined us, when he cracked open

his own beer, and we laughed as the wind—
progenitor of surfaces—carried itself across

the elegy of beveled land, each new moment
slicing into the belly of a passing cloud.

On the Roof

Everyone knows that breaths
become wreckage

falling from our bodies,
discarded and forgotten.

My brother and I smoked
often on the roof

of our father's house,
the stars fanning out,

the moon skinned
to a pale pulp.

And in the woods
along the river,

there were dead things.
Dead shadows and logs

spilling wood salt,
and a fetid confetti

of leaves. And the water
itself unfurled such a dark,

rippling flag we knew
it had been dreamed.

We drank beer
and cursed and peed

over the edge of the eaves,
and my brother asked

one night if I thought
I could kill someone—

murder him or her—
given the correct

circumstances. Later,
of course, I returned

often to that question,
imagining my brother

leaning back on the cot
in his cell, his body

lashed to the mast
of the decades,

the question hovering
with its scab. But the words,

when we were young,
seemed a blind deposition

interrogating the night,
like an exile of breaths

existing then vanishing
in air.

Rust of Rain

The white-stucco house of the girl
my brother killed sat across the street

from the park where the three of us
smoked weed sometimes in high school

and the night clouds were as thin as saplings
and the stars—shy and manifold—

undressed themselves. Often my brother
and the girl disappeared with a blanket

into the trees, where the mosquitoes anointed
their bodies in blood while I waited by the swings,

the sky secreting its juices as moonlight.
Some nights we knocked lightly on the girl's

bedroom window, and her screen lifted
to allow us to climb in, and we sat on

her floor, our voices quiet and lethargic
and bodiless. Once, after my brother

went to prison, I saw her parents wandering
down a Kmart aisle, and I fled into

a rust of rain falling from the evening sky.
Another time, in winter, I drove to the park

and studied how late-afternoon light dropped
its last stitch, studied how the purgatory

of my breaths seemed one more stupefied
otherness, something conjured and forgotten.

I tried envisioning my brother driving drunk
over railroad tracks, tried imagining the girl

dying the moment they struck the tree,
but I couldn't picture her as anywhere

except still sitting cross-legged on
her bedroom floor, in thin pajamas, or lying

with my brother on a blanket beneath
an exhumation of summer stars.

The Gift

The first time my brother fought back,
it didn't end well, which is what
he never learned, that blows returned
to our father were a gift. And then
there was the time my brother visited me
in college and stepped from one dorm
fire-escape to another, and because
he was drunk and reading the lines
on the palms of the winter sky,
he nearly fell to the death that everyone
expected. As a boy he had the habit
of chewing on the side of his thumb
until it bled, then would lean that bright
welling toward me and say *here, here*,
then would suck on its bounty like a succulent
fruit. Once our father threw him from
a rowboat into Lake Elizabeth, then beat him
about the head with an oar, but my brother
simply gave him the finger and swam away,
and my father—who admired anyone
as stupid and bullheaded as he was—laughed
and rowed beside him, pretending he might
beat him once again. And even when the expected
finally happened, my father raised a glass
after the funeral to say loudly that all those dead
motherfuckers in hell better watch out, for they
were about to get their asses kicked.

From Some Other World

The second time my brother went to prison,
I drove to Twin Falls, Idaho to visit him

for forty minutes in what reminded me
of a high school cafeteria. He'd lost

weight since I'd last seen him, and his long
hair was shaved close now to his skull,

and we spoke in uneasy sentences that seemed
to parse their passage then evaporate.

There were several subjects we avoided,
toxic memories that seemed unyielding

yet still tensile in their weight, as though
the essence of a thing were forever the shapes

into which it might be twisted. Above us, a bulb
sputtered in its wire cage, and before me

he was frenetic in his chair, impatient,
as though our time apart had become

a kind of swimming toward the lip
of a great sea. We began talking, finally,

about a time in high school when we stole
a Volkswagen and drove to Wisconsin for his

birthday, and because the drinking age
was eighteen, he stepped into the bar

while I waited in the parking lot, though every
half hour he ferried another beer bottle

inside his coat to pass it through the window
of the car. We were worried by then

about how long the vehicle had been in
our possession, so he found three college girls

who agreed to drive us back to Illinois,
and he sat in the backseat and made out

with the tallest and loudest of the three,
while I sat in front and spoke

to the driver about how she had stopped
attending classes so was flunking out,

though so far no one had thought to tell her
she was supposed to leave the dorm.

At one point the tall girl started shouting
something at my bother, which started

such a terrible row that we were evicted
ten miles from our home. And so we walked,

returning to our father's house in bright morning
to discover a small miracle: he had passed out

on the back porch and so didn't see us
coming in. Often, in the past, my brother

and I had returned to this story to share it
with our friends, describing it as some Odyssean

adventure, some fabulous trial and triumph,
but now, inside the prison, the words

no longer fit inside their skin, constructed
from some past world we had forgotten.

I spent the night in a motel in Twin Falls,
and then, come morning, visited

the Perrine Coulee Falls in a snowstorm,
watching how the water and the flakes dropped

without a moment's hesitation toward the land.
Then I drove the 1,500 miles back to Illinois—

with only three brief stops—and arrived
for my shift with twenty minutes to spare.

Riptide

My brother used to say that our father was a jackass,
though sometimes he called him a bastard instead,

or maybe a fuck-up, and somehow, over years,
the words began to feel like a great clearing,

the sort of place where you might lie on your back
on the grass and gaze at the rented clouds going by.

But there were other times when I believed the words
were waves, blue or gray rumblings lifting

themselves until the white froth foamed along
some hidden shore. My brother used to refer to our father

as though he were a riptide, this phenomenon
that could be dangerous unless you knew

the trick of it, which he did, and which he made
an effort to teach me. My first mistake, he always said,

was to imagine that a riptide had feelings or sense
and that somehow you could reason with it.

And my second mistake was to imagine that though
it might drag me under for a time it wouldn't

actually drown me. And once when I visited
my brother in prison, he pointed to his head and said

that this was where our father lived, that he grew
like lichen to cling to every thought, and that what

we felt for him was fermented love, some drunken
knuckle of affection that bruised a lip or opened

a fissure above an eye. Our father hadn't spoken to him
in years, but now my brother said he thought of the jackass

almost every day, mostly when he was taking
a shit, and I could make of that whatever I wanted.

Into the Curvature of Earth

We imagined, sometimes, that my brother
was swimming out to where there was nothing

but the tactile wheel of waves, the brine
and the wet. And in this vision he was slipping

forever into one more envelope of wave,
ranging farther and farther from his family

and friends. This was after he was out of prison
that first time, after he wouldn't respond

to any phone call or letter, and living,
we were told, in Twin Falls, Idaho,

with a pregnant addict. Often I sat
in my father's kitchen, and we discussed

my brother as though he had ventured out
into some choppy sea at night, the epithelial

moonlight so faint atop the waves it must
have seemed a dream. So when we learned

he'd been arrested once again, we imagined
the servitude of years as one more dark expanse

of liquid into which he was reaching with his arms.
And we pictured him ranging so far from shore

it was unlikely he was ever coming back,
but was leaning his weight into the rotation

of the planet, the centrifugal force of it
drawing him toward the world's lip.

Flashing

I was up on my roof in Illinois,
checking why the flashing
around the chimney seemed to have
so little impact on keeping out the rain,
when the F.B.I. stopped by the house
to ask when I had last seen
my brother. At first their words
were shouted up to the roof,
and my words were shouted down
to the grass, but then I eased
down the ladder and invited the men
into my kitchen, where I offered them
coffee and told them I hadn't seen him
since a few days after Christmas,
and I was pretty certain he had long ago
left town. I didn't ask what he'd done
this time, but instead found myself
telling a story to the agents about a day
when we were kids and my brother
sneaked into the neighbor's kitchen
and stole a pie. Mrs. Orlen
was always baking cookies and cakes
and chocolate pastries, and often
we would climb the backyard ramp
to her kitchen door, would be invited in
to stand beside where she was maneuvering
her wheelchair, and we accepted whatever
sweet tidbits she handed over. So always
we perked up when the baking smells
of flour and sugar came wafting through
the open windows of our house,
and on this occasion my brother crept up
the ramp while I watched, and a minute later
he came running back with the entire pie
in his hands. It turned out to be rhubarb,
though, so my brother threw most of it
over the fence to where a neighbor's dog
was always barking, though the dog
wouldn't eat the pie either but simply nosed

at the crust. Why I told this story to the F.B.I.
I don't actually know, but both agents
nodded solemnly, as though this
were crucial information for their case,
then we shook hands and I followed them
out to their car. And before they climbed in,
I pointed out that my brother wasn't
actually all that bad, not when you got
to know him, and he had his good traits, too,
and the men nodded solemnly before they drove
away, and I nodded solemnly in return, and a few
days later they must have found him, for my aunt
phoned to say that he was once again in jail.

Letters from Prison

I

I remember being home after so long away. Those first weeks. The years I'd been away like a slow fan on a high ceiling in dead summer. But it didn't seem like home. It seemed like a memory, a dream version of a past and forgotten life, as though I had gained hazy access to the thoughts and long-ago experiences of someone who was no longer me, or maybe never was, if that makes sense.

Most of the time, I felt as though I were actually still lying in my cot at McRae, there in the lost center of Illinois, there with only the pink of my closed eyelids to keep me company. For I had learned in that place to live behind my eyes, beneath my ribs, hidden in the deep pocket of it all.

So it felt wrong, just wrong, to be back in the house where I had once gone running as a child, where I had argued with our father as a teen, when you and I would climb on the roof and smoke and bitch about him. And I remember one particular afternoon in those first weeks when he was off at work, and when I—the ex-con up to no good, he surely feared—was left by myself. This was a different kind of boredom than prison, but no less oppressive. I stepped out on the front porch and saw, up on the raised road—I had forgotten how quiet it was this far from town, how desolate, like something that had long ago stopped breathing—a dead crow at the roadside. Probably it had been struck by a passing car. There, in bright sunlight, was the black of its body. There, in bright sunlight, was the shroud of closed wings.

And as I lit my cigarette and watched, a pickup went whooshing by at maybe sixty or seventy, speeding in the direction of the railroad tracks and the river, and the crow, so still before, suddenly twitched as though coming back to life, as though its wings had remembered what it meant to be inside the world and planned to lift from the earth and back into the sky, to become a crow again that I could watch oar away.

It was all an illusion, of course. That little trick the eyes play on the mind. And I remember thinking: *That's me, that's me.*

II

Something I should explain. It is possible to hold two opposing beliefs in the mind at the same moment. To clutch both fervently. We are talking preacher beliefs here, down-on-your-knees beliefs, rock-core certainty. This was after I had moved from Dad's house into your apartment. When I began working at Ike's as a cook. Before I broke parole and moved with Brigit to Twin Falls (sore subject, I know). There was a little window of time then, a sliver in the fabric of my days, an envelope into which I had slipped. I was trying, for once, to be the GOOD BROTHER. Working hard at my shifts. Talking the talk. Yes, we went drinking sometimes, but did you notice the moderation with which I sipped my Coors? Not Pabst Blue Ribbon, like Dad the whole time we were growing up, but Coors Light, of all things. Did you notice how I labored to keep my voice on an even keel? We had been raised with such emotional weather in the household, after all—both Dad and me—so now I was trying to stop it in its tracks. Did you realize I wanted to sound like you, was trying to be you? You were always the one who seemed to think in childhood that the waters around our boat were calm. I envied that. It infuriated me. Didn't you understand that our lives—including yours—were taking on water? We were going to be capsized? Anyway, we went out drinking on those nights when we were roomies. And there you sat, tugging at the label on your bottle, your eyes looking sleepy. You yawned while talking about work, and then, barely inebriated, barely anything, we went back to your apartment and fell asleep before midnight, monks well-rested for morning prayers.

And what were the contradictory thoughts I clutched tightly to my chest while I lay in bed, unable to sleep, and gazed at the lights from passing cars sweeping their sad existence across the ceiling? It was simple enough:

I will never go back to prison, will live, as they say, on the straight and narrow.

And: *I will surely go back to prison, for this is my fate, for this is who I am, for being doomed is the one thing I have always counted on.*

III

A quick story about summer camp. For that was how McRae struck me at first. Though, to be sure, an awful summer camp. The worst ever. A summer camp in hell. *Don't send your kids there, Folks, unless you really don't like them.* I expected, before I arrived, cell doors to clang shut after me, enclosing me with finality. I expected cinder block walls with blood stains from skulls being cracked against them. I expected one high window in the cell, far out of reach, letting in the most sickly cyst of daylight I had ever seen. I expected the shaved heads of my fellow convicts, the open toilet in the cell where my cellmate—sadist, pervert—would make swamp smells that would try to suffocate me. But what I didn't expect was rows of cots laid out in our open cell block like a small gymnasium, little cubbyholes where we kept our few belongings, the communal bathrooms with rows of open stalls and showers. What I didn't expect was how juvenile my fellow inmates seemed. Stupid jokes. Pranks. Giggling. Mixed with sudden, terrifying rages of violence. No impulse control. None. Goofy kids with violent tempers and far too much time on their hands. What I didn't expect was the long and tedious hours in the TV room, arguing over what to watch next, though none of us really much liked any of it. And the "jobs." The worst and most stupid and pointless forms of menial labor. But mostly what I didn't expect? The big topper? I remember being awakened on my first "morning" at McRae. Awakened by the bright lights coming on...not that they ever let it get very dark. Just the difference between low light and spotlight. In the night a cockroach had gone running across my arm while I was sleeping, awakening me. In the night I had heard what I had thought were probably mice in the walls beside my ear. In the night I had heard snoring, inmates muttering in their sleep, everyone rolling over in their cots. In the night I had been certain, at one point, that the inmate in the bunk across from me was jerking off. In the night I had been unable to make up my mind about whether to start laughing or crying. It was that bad. That surreal.

Then suddenly the lights came on. Time to get up. Breakfast time. *It was not yet even four in the morning.* 3:45. Why? Overcrowding, of course. Have to start breakfast early so everyone can file into the limited cafeteria space. So lucky me: our cell block was first shift. We stumbled like zombies. We pushed our plastic trays and accepted the offerings of slop. Yes, it was bad. Imagine the most tasteless food you have ever consumed in your life...then mix it with sawdust. Cardboard. Dirt. The food was so boring that it was difficult to understand why it felt so heavy in the belly, so much like a slab of cement, a brick.

So the story I am taking my slow, sweet time to tell? That first morning over breakfast, I was hopelessly nervous to make "friends," hopelessly nervous to "fit in" (oh God, grade school again), and I was already realizing that being in prison was like being a kid once more. Your parents, the guards, told you exactly what to do and exactly when to do it. And mostly you obeyed. What choice did you have? Mostly you accepted being infantilized (aren't you impressed that your brother, whose highest grade in school was a C+, knows that word?). Only very occasionally did you rebel, and then, mostly, it was simply to throw a tantrum for a few lost moments. Then life went on. That's the discouraging part. Nothing changed in prison. It was the same, same, every day. Exactly the same.

So the story? I sat with a group I was hoping to befriend—I chose them practically at random—sat with a wary smile, a half-nod, and what were they talking about? What did criminals talk about at such at early hour, long before the sun had bothered dragging its old body into the sky? I kid you not: CONSTIPATION. How bad it was. Apparently an epidemic. All of them. Comparing stories like the size of fish caught by fishermen. *Once I went nine days*, one said. *That's bullshit*, another said. *You can't go nine days. You'd explode.* And the first one said, *It felt like I was going to.* And then, to my astonishment, they all started talking about their best bowel movements in prison. The ones where they shat like motherfuckers. Their expressions were blissful. I am not lying, not exaggerating. It was like teens bragging about getting some sweet little piece of ass. But this was about shit. Emptying themselves. Stopping up toilet bowls. Overflowing. And I began wondering in that moment if, somehow, I was wrong about prison after all, that it wasn't a camp for children but more like a nursing home for senior citizens. It was a strange moment. Bizarre. And I think, if I am honest, that it colored how I felt about prison from that day forward. How it was a place unto itself, unlike any other, unlike anything possible.

And then one of them asked me—and I was so pleased to be included—*So, hey, how about you, New Guy, you pretty regular?*

IV

There is something else I never told you. I went to see her house. Maybe five times. All within those few months before I broke parole. I parked across the street one evening and looked out from the park. I tried to remember. I knew, of course, that Connie's parents had moved to Wisconsin, that I was staring at an empty shell. That was how it felt, at least. There was the limestone exterior. There were the green shutters and the green front door. There was the slope of the roof. There was, out back—though I didn't walk there—the window where I always tapped my knuckles against glass, where Connie would climb out or I would climb in. It's terrible, of course. In prison I thought about those times when she dragged me through that window. The salty-skin memories. The slick-body memories. Friction. Was it unforgiveable to think sex thoughts about a girl who was dead? And because of me?

So why did I want to stare at her house? Was I saying I was sorry? Was I telling her that I drank only in moderation now, only on boring nights with my little brother? Boring sips? Was I telling her it should have been me? Was I remembering flying over those railroad tracks by the County Fairgrounds (I drove there occasionally, too, after I was home from prison, since I am confessing to it all)? Was I remembering the snow falling out of the sky after we struck the tree? I believed in those minutes after the crash that it was ash coming down. I believed that the clouds and the stars had burned away into nothing and were falling on the distortions of the mangled car. I believed that we were anointed in blood, were a strange blood sacrifice. I believed in the sounds of moaning, though I couldn't tell if it was Connie moaning or me.

The truth? It was none of that. That's not why I wanted to look again at Connie's house. Of course I felt guilty. Of course I was sorry about what she had lost—how can you make up for taking everything?— what her parents had lost. But I kept gazing at the house because I needed something, something I hoped seeing the house would give me. I wanted to believe that what had happened had happened. That going to prison had happened. That being out had happened. That my life was happening. That trying never to get locked up again was happening. And that weird part was that each time I stood there I believed it.

V

A quick childhood memory. You must have been seven, me eight. Dad driving. His silver pickup. The bad muffler. Remember? I am sure he had been drinking. Probably was drinking right there in the truck as he drove. Do you remember how he would sometimes let us sit in his lap and steer? Do you remember how loud he'd turn up the radio to his country songs? Remember how he kept the window open on his side, even in winter? Anyhow, we were making too much noise or something, or goofing off, and his arm came sweeping out and got us both. I don't remember anything else about that day. But I see that big arm of his coming toward us. Do you remember how I used to tell you to watch for his mouth to grow hard? To watch for the sudden twitching of his shoulders? That was the warning sign. Only neither of us saw it this time. That beefy slab came toward us, catching us both across the face. You were about elbow distance away, and I was fist. Suddenly there was just that loud thud, the seizure of pain. But here's the part that has stayed with me. The little miracle. Something to rival Jesus curing lepers, the five loaves and the two fish. I looked at you, and your nose was bleeding. I touched the back of my wrist to my nose, and I was bleeding, too. That motherfucker got us both *with one blow*. I admired him in that moment. He was a little god. I was fucking impressed. How warped is that?

VI

Let's cut to the chase: I know you blamed Brigit for my skipping parole. Hell, I blamed her, too. But it was my fault. We all know it was my fault. I still remember you warning me…in your indirect way. You are the king, little brother, of saying things sideways, saying things with the real meaning buried somewhere underneath, peeking out between closed fingers.

"She sure does know how to have a good time," you said.

And what did that mean? Do you want me to translate it? You meant, *Are you out of your fucking mind? Do you really think hanging around with a drunk and a druggie is your best choice? Is that going to help? Are you sure that wild is what you need at this point in your life? Don't you think she's the exact fucking opposite of what you need? And you're okay with the fact that she's been in the system, too? So you think check kiting and fraud are a good match? You think two screwups cancel each other out, so you'll be fine? Are you really going to be dumb all your life? Is that what's going on?*

But here's what you never knew. That's not how I saw her. I saw her, I think, as SECOND CHANCE. See those caps. Not little chance but the real deal. Why? She reminded me of Connie. Sweet trouble. Beautiful trouble. Innocent trouble. I looked at her and thought, *This is how Connie would have turned out*. I don't mean the superficial things. Connie wasn't that skinny, for one thing, and never would have been. And I can't see Connie with that many tattoos and such a bounty of piercings. And that short little black hair, weird little bangs. Connie? Of course not.

But the essence. Their deep-down truthness. Brigit was Connie's doppelganger. Not in any creepy way. But in a sad way, a tragic way. It took me years to realize this, but I had taken all of my convoluted and fucked-up feelings of need and love and guilt and loneliness for Connie and had swallowed them far down into my belly, where I didn't have to look at them. They lived there, stewing in the juices. I know that is a weird metaphor. I do. Then Brigit was in my life and I upchucked it all back into the world. Except imagine that upchucking could be beautiful. That's how it felt. So what am I trying to say? I loved Brigit. I loved her through all of it. I know you didn't think I was listening to you. I know you believed I was avoiding the indirection of your statements.

"I don't think I've ever met anyone quite like her."

Translation: *She is insane. Absolutely INSANE. She is going to drag you down with her. She is going to land you back in prison. Both of you. Is that what you want? Are you really going to fuck up again? Is that your plan for your life?*

Do you know the first time I slept with her? It was within an hour after I first met her. I never told you that part. I told you how she came by Ike's near closing time, looking for a waitressing gig. I told you I was on my way out and we struck up a conversation. I offered her a cigarette. She rode her bike to the restaurant. I don't mean a motorcycle. A kid's bike. This grown woman with wrinkles starting in at the corners of her eyes. It turned out she was about four years ahead of us in school. Knew some of the same people. And what did she tell me? I never told you this part either. She was already saying that her sister was living in Twin Falls, and she was thinking about heading out. She just wanted the waitressing job long enough to make enough for the bus. I asked her what she knew about Twin Falls, or Idaho in general, and she said: *Nothing. Absolutely nothing. That's what I like about it.*

And I said, *Maybe I'll go with you. I don't know anything about it either.*

And she said, *It would give us something to talk about.*

And I said, *You've hit my area of expertise. I can go on and on about how little I know.*

So I invited her back to my place (okay, your place). And we both knew it was going to happen. And we both knew it was "inappropriate." And it was like we were saying to each other: *We share this in common. We both don't do rules very well. We never put our toys away as kids. We don't always wash our hands after going to the bathroom. Don't even necessarily remember to flush. We leave dishes in the sink, or maybe on the table. We annoy people around us. We are inconsiderate. We aren't always very nice. Okay, we are jackasses at times. We have bad tempers. We do bad things. But we aren't bad people. At least we don't think we are. We think we deserve to be loved. We think we deserve happiness. We think we mean well, or try to mean well.*

I loved her. I know how bad that sounds. She spread her legs in that first hour, and I thought, *I am going to be with her forever. This is the woman I want. This is the woman who can make me whole. This is the woman who can destroy me. The is her, her.*

VII

Another prison story from McCrae. This one pretty funny. An inmate stabbed me with a shard of glass that—or so the rumor went—came from a green Perrier bottle. Did I ever tell you this one? Afterwards, everyone kept asking the same question. It wasn't, *Are you okay, okay?* It was, *How did he get a Perrier bottle? Who drinks Perrier? How did it get smuggled in?* Then, later, *How do you know it was Perrier. It was just green glass. That could have been anything. Who was the one who said it was Perrier?*

And why was I stabbed? The answer will tell you everything about prison life. The inmate who stabbed me was Frank Becker. But everyone called him Boris. Apparently after some tennis player. But since a lot of people at the prison had never heard of Boris Becker, and didn't know he was German, everything started calling Frank "The Russian." Or sometimes The Rusky. That last name was probably the most common after a time. But that wasn't why he stabbed me. One day there were maybe nine of us in the showers, and someone said loudly that we were the ugliest collection of naked human flesh he had ever seen, and if he'd ever thought about turning gay in prison that the sight of us had just talked him out of it. I don't even remember who said that, but then all the rest of us started saying out loud the particularly unsavory features of the naked inmates around us. And what did I say? I said that the hair on Rusky's ass looked like a Chia Pet, which started everybody laughing hysterically. So did Rusky attack me then? No. Apparently, instead, he seethed over it, bided his time. Apparently my telling him that his butt was hairy was more than he could bear as a human being, and worth risking adding significant time to his sentence. Some slights simply can't go unanswered.

So maybe a week letter he attacked me in the hallway outside the TV room. We were walking past each her.

"Hey, Rusky," I said.

And he said, "I'm going to kill you."

Then he was slicing at me with that green glass. And he stabbed me in the forearm that I lifted to project my body. And the shard went deep into the flesh. And Rusky cut one of his fingers in the process as well.

And both of us got clocked by the guards when they broke up our tussle. And I ended up with nine stitches in my arm.

But for weeks afterwards, the only topic of conversation at the prison was about Perrier. Had anyone ever tried it? Wasn't it just expensive water? It had bubbles, didn't it? Why? Who wanted to drink water with bubbles? What was the point? From France? Didn't only rich people drink it? How had Ruksy gotten hold of it? Could it have been some other green bottle instead? Really…who liked Perrier?

VIII

It is strange to write these words. *I have killed two people in my life. Murdered. Two.* It sounds, as I think it inside my head, like something a child would write. When we are young we imagine that our lives will spread out like some great and endless sea, stretching out and out to where the horizon and the great rolls of waves blur into a kind of intermediacy. We think, as children, that a life is a container so large that surely we will fill it with a little bit of everything. We will be saints, criminals, baseball players, actors, soldiers, lovers, world travelers, philosophers, parents, senators. And in that vision, two murders might seem fairly small. It's not, after all, *I will kill nine people in my life. I will have seventy-two lovers. I will be a king and a pauper. I will live atop mountains and in dry deserts and in maybe even, someday, on the moon.*

It is only when we grow older that we learn the truth about our lives. They are like one of those airplane bathrooms that feel, when you stand in one, like an upright coffin. We live our lives in tight spaces, under the stricture of hard limits, our choices forever narrowing and narrowing until we are lying in a cell one day and this thought occurs to us:

Inside of me is a skeleton. Bones. This is all I have. They will outlive me. I cannot escape them. Ever.

And by this reckoning, of course, two murders sounds massive. It is a personal ocean. It is the personal distance between here and the moon, here and the stars. The number is so large it swallows everything.

IX

Another childhood memory, though not one you are likely to remember. A Mom memory. We were at a restaurant. It might have been Burger King, though it could have been something else. Arby's? Anyway, I remember that it was raining. How come I remember that? I remember that the window next to our booth seemed to be crying or maybe drooling. Do you hear how often I keep saying "remember"? When you think about it, all our lives are like standing at the back of a boat and watching the wake spread behind us. We think we are that wake. We think we are the foaming water. And I remember our mother telling our dad to calm down. Just like that. *Calm down, calm down.* I can almost hear her voice. I know you wish that you had actual memories of her before she died and left us alone, instead of just memories of being told about her. Dad was in one of his moody states that evening. He had been cheerful and talkative, telling stories, going on and on, and then the switch had flipped. (I know that switch well...he handed it down to me. The switch that goes: *I am happy, everything is great, I am glad to be with all of you to I hate you, I hate everything and everyone, I am furious, my anger is a fire, see it flaring up, see it trying to consume you, too?*).

"It's okay," Mom was saying. "It's okay."

It made things worse, of course. He flung his sandwich at her. That's why I think I remember it. The bun tumbling through the air, striking her chest. Lettuce dribbling down. Ketchup. A pickle, I think. I'm not sure. Just that all of it was now a Rorschach design on her chest. Then he was up, storming from the restaurant. Mom was calling after him. Mom was frantic. Then we saw him walking through the onslaught of rain, climbing into his pickup. We saw him driving off. And Mom was saying, *He left us, what are we going to do, how are we going to get home, what if he drives too fast in the rain, I hope he's all right, I hope he comes back.*

And you, the calm one in the family, were quietly eating French fries. One after the other. Shoving them in your mouth. And I kept thinking: *I hope Dad dies on the road, I hope he never comes back, I hope he keeps driving till he falls in the ocean.*

Which I didn't mean, of course. Which I did mean, of course. Which was beyond any real kind of meaning. I was just a kid, that is. That meaning said, *I ache, I hurt, I want.*

X

I know how you imagined my life in Twin Falls. Breaking parole. Taking off on a Greyhound with Brigit. I see you and Dad standing in our childhood backyard, gazing out at the raised railroad tracks and the river. The two of you are slowly shaking your heads. *How can one person make so many bad decisions in his life?* The truth? You were right, of course. Everything you imagined was the case. Probably a lot of things you never got around to imagining. Brigit was the gasoline and I was the match. I was the gasoline and Brigit was the match. Together we were a beautiful and destructive conflagration. Falling down drinking? Of course. Drugs? You bet. Selling drugs? Absolutely. A little B & E? We were game. Shoplifting? We were pros. Larceny? Do bears shit in the woods? Domestic violence with each other? How else do crazy people express love? So, yes, we were the exact shit show you imagined…except worse. Twin Falls was a disaster. In every way. Twice on Sundays.

But here's the thing that's much harder to explain. We knew, of course, that we were almost always on the wrong side of things, were walking that tightrope and sometimes falling off. But did we think of ourselves as criminals? Did we think of ourselves as off the rails?

Of course not. We thought of ourselves as…wait for it…OUTLAWS. There is a fine American tradition in flouting the rules. Conformists are saps. We were cool, Baby. We were dreamers. We were living it. Who doesn't romanticize an outlaw? And we were in it together. Brigit and I were living the life of movies and Dad's country music songs. Brigit and I were living real life, gritty life, down-and-dirty life.

But we weren't bad people. Nope. Maybe we did some bad things, but that didn't define us. What defined us were our hearts, which were good. We were good people, despite it all. We were just like everyone else. Trying our best. Fucking up now and then. Human, in other words. We still missed our mommies (truly, Brother, truly), still felt like lost little kids in our hearts, still gripped each with desperate love when we had sex. That was life in Idaho. That was who we would be forever. We thought that. There's a line from Hemingway you used to quote sometimes. You see, I did listen when you talked. Despite evidence to the contrary.

Isn't it pretty to think so?

XI

Centennial Waterfront Park. Snake River. Brigit and I went canoeing there once. Our second summer in Idaho. We were flush with cash for once. Were feeling chipper. It was a hopelessly hot summer day, and it felt good to have the sun falling on us, baking us, forcing its warmth deep into our essences. That's how it felt. Cooking the alcoholism right out of us (though we drank beer as we worked the canoe paddles). We stripped down to as much as skin as we could. We studied the gray little wrinkles of river beneath us, always on the go, always heading out in the same direction, the current like a slap-in-the-face metaphor, but still beautiful, serene. Places like that take you outside your own life, your own body, even as you feel your own legs and arms more fully, realizing, like some weird drug-induced epiphany, that they belong to *you, you*. We paddled and paddled and pointed at rock obelisks and tabletops and sudden patches of vivid green. We felt the breezes take the sweat on our skin and turn it into miniature air-conditioners. We spoke in voices like a benediction, like a fucking religious experience. We had a picnic lunch with our canoe dragged up part way to shore. Ate in a crazy little copse of trees. Some almost shade. Then fucked. Had sex. Made love. Did it. Bedded each other without the bed. I should probably say how great it was. Pyrotechnics. Fireworks. But no. It was better than that. The best ever. Why? It was sweet. It was gentle. It was affectionate. We breathed deeply. We said nice things to each other. Not dirty but caring. Like we were some normal couple. And there were the sounds of birds around us, a susurration, a white noise, a dream erasure. Then we got back in the canoe and paddled off toward the rest of our lives.

So why am I sharing this story? I think about it often. Prison the second time around. What's it like? *Second verse same as the first.* Except in Idaho instead of Illinois. And the difference? Only one that matters. I have memories now of Snake River, how it sank its fangs of love into our bodies...at least that one day. Is that enough? Truly, Brother, I think about Brigit every day of my life. Think about her and Connie and climbing through the window and Snake River. I imagine I am on a raft now, floating across the metaphor of years, the Snake River of decades. The water, beneath me, is not quite lucid, not quite opaque. That's a metaphor for something, I guess. You can't see to the bottom but can almost imagine that you can. You keep expecting to, in other words. So I walk around this prison or try to sleep at night, and what goes through my mind? The way those paddles felt when we dipped them into the resistance of the river. The way a life feels when you dip your breaths into the resistance of your body. I don't know how to say it. It is beyond saying. That's the conclusion I have come to. Why do all of us talk so much in our lives? Why do we put so much down on a page? Simple. Because we never get it right. Each new word is a revision of the one that came before. One more attempt. Failed, of course. All life is failure. That's my philosophy. Maybe it's self-serving…a way of making an excuse. I worry that you will read it that way. But it's not how I mean it. Honestly.

Let me put it plainly. I confess, as they say, but don't ever let anyone convince you that it is good for the soul. Yep. I killed her. The woman I loved in my life above all others. Shot her in the head. Yep. (I write that word in that way to shock…but it's meant more to shock me, little brother, than you.) The story? I don't believe in stories. Not the kind where you say this-happened-then-that, and this-was-why. Those stories lie. All stories lie. But what other way is there to tell any story? We were both drunk out of our minds. Yep, yep, yep. We were arguing. So what happened (see, I can't escape the story-ness of it, even though every story is a lie)? She told me she was leaving me. I should have laughed, of course. How many times had she said that? How many times had I said it to her? It was our favorite song. *Oh,* we would sing together, *let's break up, let's call it quits, let's say sayonara.* We even did split a few times. Briefly. Even did fuck around a little. Both of us. Huge rows over it. White-hot jealousy. Blue-hot jealousy. So I went into the bedroom and expected to see her packing. Planned to help her. Planned to say good riddens. Our favorite dance. We had practiced the choreography to perfection. But this time, to my shock, she was sitting on the rim of the bathtub, clutching her face with her hands. Crying. Bawling her eyes out, as they say. And here's the thing. Here's the truth. I suddenly realized that she meant it this time. She was leaving me for good. It was over. And I was drunk, drunk (no excuses, just a fact). And the automatic was in my belt (long story, long sad story), and I pulled it out and shot her. Yep. In the head. She fell back in the bathtub. Instant red. Deep dark, but bright. Yep. I actually watched it swirling down the drain. I was planning to shoot myself, too. That was the plan. Climb in beside her. Both us swirling together.

XII

So why didn't I? That's the million-dollar question that no one would pay even a dime for. The answer is obvious, though not the obvious one you think. Even in that moment, I couldn't believe it. Even when I knew she was already gone, I kept expecting her to stand up in the tub and curse me, tell me what a jackass I was, punch me hard, tell me it hurt, really hurt...let's go have a drink. I phoned for an ambulance. Even though I knew she was dead. I said she'd been shot. I said I'd shot her... even though I knew what that meant. Even though I knew the police would be coming. And then I lost my nerve again, and ran. Ran out of the apartment complex. But I had forgotten the car keys. Was afraid to go back to get them. So ran. Ran. Was arrested not even an hour later. How about that for an outlaw story? I was sitting on a curb by a gas station, in plain sight, when the squad car pulled up. Yep. The outlaw lay flat on his belly and put his hands behind his head. The outlaw knew the drill. The outlaw was bawling like a baby when they put him in the backseat.

And he closed his eyes in that car and thought about what? I wish I could say that I thought about Snake River, about sex amid the birds, about love. About how I wished I hadn't done it. But nope. I thought about that fucking crow from so many years earlier. The twitching of wings. Their flutter. Even though it was already dead. Even though—for all the difference it made—it might have been dead a million years.

Dream Play

CAST

FATHER

BIG BROTHER

LITTLE BROTHER

DEAD MOTHER

ACT ONE

The family is sitting at the kitchen table, eating breakfast. The kitchen window looks out on open fields and far horizons. There is almost a river, almost train tracks. It is bleak morning, despair-gray. Father is hungover. He is all angry slump, belligerent stasis. An invisible collection of beer cans lies scattered across a back porch that can't be seen. Big Brother and Little Brother are sometimes children and sometimes teenagers and sometimes adults. Occasionally they are all three at once. Mother is always dead, though often she looks up as though startled, or pours herself a little cereal for her bowl, or gazes forlornly out the window. It is raining. It is snowing. The sun shines. At first the four talk without sound, but then, all at once, their voices are audible.

FATHER: I've had about enough.

BIG BROTHER: *Feigning shock.* We didn't do anything.

FATHER: I told you to keep your voices down. I told you I had a headache.

BIG BROTHER: We can't talk?

FATHER: *Silence. His eyes glare. His eyes say: go ahead, see what happens if one more word arrives.*

DEAD MOTHER: *Silence. She appears concerned.*

BIG BROTHER: *Silence.*

LITTLE BROTHER: *Silence.*

A minute passes. A month passes. A year passes. A decade passes. Time is so fuzzy that it's hard to tell. There is mute silence at the table, until, once more, the sound is turned up without warning.

BIG BROTHER: *Stirring his spoon aimlessly in his cereal. Glancing at his brother. Speaking softly.* You done? Let's go.

LITTLE BROTHER: Go where?

BIG BROTHER: *A voice like the softest of breaking glass.* Anywhere. Somewhere on our bikes.

LITTLE BROTHER: Okay.

BIG BROTHER: *Looking at his dad. Waiting. The bear of the father seems to be hibernating. In this moment, Father is an actual bear. Big Brother looks back at Little Brother. Rising, he mouths the words.* Let's go.

LITTLE BROTHER: *Rising, too.* Okay.

FATHER: *Opening his eyes.* Where are you going?

BIG BROTHER: Out to play.

FATHER: What about the dishes?

BIG BROTHER: We'll do them when we get back.

FATHER: Now.

Suddenly, without transition, the boys are at the sink, running water, laughing, talking loudly in words that are unintelligible. Soap suds fall around them like snow.

FATHER: What did I tell you about being quiet?

BIG BROTHER: *Giving his father's back the finger.* Sorry.

LITTLE BROTHER: *Trying not to giggle.* Sorry.

DEAD MOTHER: *Silence. Looking concerned.*

FATHER: *Rising.* Are you two getting mouthy with me?

BIG BROTHER: No!

LITTLE BROTHER: No!

DEAD MOTHER: *Silence! Very concerned!*

FATHER: Maybe we should discuss it.

BIG BROTHER: No!

LITTLE BROTHER: No!

DEAD MOTHER: *No!*

Sounds of the boys crying. A minute passes. A year. A lifetime. Then all of them are back sitting at the table, eating cereal once again. The knob turns and their voices come on.

FATHER: *Looking at his older son.* Do you know how disappointed I am? You are worthless. You are a murderer. What's wrong with you? I always knew you were trouble. I always knew you would end up in prison. You are a terrible person. It's good your mother never saw you grow up. That's all I have to say. I should have drowned you. Like they do with pups that are born wrong. At least your mother never saw this.

FATHER, BIG BROTHER, and LITTLE BROTHER all look at DEAD MOTHER, who gazes down at her hands.

BIG BROTHER *(he is young here...nine? ten?)*: Dismayed, perplexed. Stop it, Dad.

FATHER: You are talking back?

BIG BROTHER: Why are you calling me names?

FATHER: Because I know everything.

BIG BROTHER *(much older now)*: Maybe I should beat the shit of you.

FATHER: You could try.

BIG BROTHER: Maybe I will murder you, too.

FATHER: Wouldn't surprise me. Go ahead and try.

LITTLE BROTHER: *Silence.*

DEAD MOTHER: *Rising to look out the window.*

FATHER: We have this hatred in us, Son. You and me. I admire that.

BIG BROTHER: You admire me?

FATHER: You're actually my favorite. Don't tell your brother.

LITTLE BROTHER: *Looking down.*

DEAD MOTHER: *Almost running her almost hand through her younger son's hair.*

FATHER: That's why I should have drowned you as a pup. Taken you to the river. Or out back with a shotgun. Would have been a mercy on us all.

BIG BROTHER: *Rising.* Maybe I'll drown you in the river.

FATHER: *Rising.* You could try.

There are fires in the distance outside the windows. Smoke everywhere. It fills the kitchen, too. There are the sounds of flying fists striking flesh, sounds of grunts, sounds of curses, sounds of moans.

Then the sounds stop, the smoke clears, and everyone is back at the table, gazing into cereal bowls.

ACT TWO

BIG BROTHER and LITTLE BROTHER are sitting on the roof, smoking cigarettes. DEAD MOTHER is nowhere to be seen. FATHER is a floating cloud passing across the moon. The moon behind that cloud is a skull. Little flares of orange when the brothers inhale are beacons.

LITTLE BROTHER: What's it like?

BIG BROTHER: What kind of question is that?

LITTLE BROTHER: I want to know.

BIG BROTHER: *Shrugging.* It's pretty good.

LITTLE BROTHER: Just good?

BIG BROTHER: I don't know. Why are you asking this? You sound like a fucking idiot.

LITTLE BROTHER: I want to know.

BIG BROTHER: Then try it yourself.

LITTLE BROTHER: Please tell me. How many times have you done it?

BIG BROTHER: I don't know.

LITTLE BROTHER: Five? Ten?

BIG BROTHER: I'm not counting.

LITTLE BROTHER: She takes her clothes off?

BIG BROTHER: What do you think?

LITTLE BROTHER: What does it feel like?

BIG BROTHER: It feels like what it feels like. Okay?

Their cigarettes are fireflies. Flaring and flaring. It's hard to know how much time has passed. Time is a firefly.

LITTLE BROTHER: What's it like?

BIG BROTHER: What kind of question is that?

LITTLE BROTHER: I want to know.

BIG BROTHER: *Shrugging.* It's okay.

LITTLE BROTHER: Okay? Really?

BIG BROTHER: I don't know. Why are you asking? You sound retarded.

LITTLE BROTHER: I want to know.

BIG BROTHER: Then get arrested yourself.

LITTLE BROTHER: Please tell me. How does it feel?

BIG BROTHER: Prison is boring. Just boring.

LITTLE BROTHER: That's it?

BIG BROTHER: Yes.

LITTLE BROTHER: And you're never going back?

BIG BROTHER: What do you think?

LITTLE BROTHER: I don't know.

BIG BROTHER: Okay then. Okay.

Cigarettes are fireflies. Flaring and flaring. It's hard to know how much time has passed. Time is a firefly.

LITTLE BROTHER: What's it like?

BIG BROTHER: What kind of question is that?

LITTLE BROTHER: I want to know.

BIG BROTHER: It's terrible.

LITTLE BROTHER: Just terrible?

BIG BROTHER: The worst ever. Why are you asking? You sound retarded.

LITTLE BROTHER: I want to know.

BIG BROTHER: Then murder someone yourself.

LITTLE BROTHER: Please tell me. How does it feel?

BIG BROTHER: *Silence.*

DEAD MOTHER: *Nowhere in sight. Silence.*

FATHER: *Passing in front of the moon. Silence.*

LITTLE BROTHER: Do you wish you could take it back?

BIG BROTHER: Of course.

LITTLE BROTHER: But you can't take it back?

BIG BROTHER: What do you think?

LITTLE BROTHER: I don't think you can.

BIG BROTHER: Okay then. Okay.

Cigarettes turn into fireflies and fly away.

ACT THREE

BIG BROTHER is lying on his prison cot. LITTLE BROTHER isn't there. DEAD MOTHER isn't there. FATHER isn't there. They are talking.

BIG BROTHER: Do you believe in prayers?

FATHER: No.

DEAD MOTHER: *Silence.*

LITTLE BROTHER: No.

BIG BROTHER: Do you believe in prayers?

FATHER: Maybe.

DEAD MOTHER: *Silence.*

LITTLE BROTHER: Maybe.

BIG BROTHER: I worry sometimes they get caught once they leave your mouth. You pray and the words go floating toward the ceiling. But what if they just bump there? You know how moths batter at a light? What if the prayers just bump against the ceiling?

FATHER: That sounds stupid.

DEAD MOTHER: *Silence.*

LITTLE BROTHER: I don't know.

BIG BROTHER: Or what if they make it through the ceiling but get caught in a cloud? Or some passing bird gets the prayer trapped in its wing? Or the prayer just tires out and falls back to the ground.

FATHER: You're an idiot.

DEAD MOTHER: *Silence.*

LITTLE BROTHER: No one knows.

BIG BROTHER: And even if it does get all the way to God, what then? How many prayers does He hear? It must be like so many bees buzzing in a hive. Does it even matter to Him? Really?

FATHER: I wish you would stop talking. I have a headache.

DEAD MOTHER: *Silence.*

LITTLE BROTHER: *Silence.*

BIG BROTHER: Does anything really even matter? I have another question, too. Do the dead forgive us?

Everyone looks at DEAD MOTHER.

FATHER: No.

DEAD MOTHER: *Silence.*

LITTLE BROTHER: Maybe.

BIG BROTHER: And if everything is so perfect in heaven, wouldn't forgiveness be part of that?

FATHER: No.

DEAD MOTHER: *Silence.*

LITTLE BROTHER: Yes.

BIG BROTHER: Do you want to hear a funny story? When I was a kid I got sick one time at the County Fair. I threw up behind the Tilt-A-Whirl. And do you know what I remember thinking? I was fascinated with the idea that God was inside us all. And I remember it occurred to me that maybe I had just upchucked God, that what I was seeing in the grass was the Holy Father. It freaked me out.

FATHER: You really are an idiot.

DEAD MOTHER: *Silence.*

LITTLE BROTHER: I don't remember you throwing up. Was I there?

BIG BROTHER: Do you know the point of the story, though?

FATHER: I don't give a shit.

DEAD MOTHER: *Silence.*

LITTLE BROTHER: No.

BIG BROTHER: I don't either. That's the part that upsets me. What if there's no point to any story?

FATHER: Then suck it up.

DEAD MOTHER: *Silence.*

LITTLE BROTHER: *Silence.*

BIG BROTHER: What if we don't have a choice in any of this anyway? If everything we are is determined by something outside us? Some fate?

FATHER: Then you suck it up.

DEAD MOTHER: *Silence.*

LITTLE BROTHER: It'll be okay. I promise.

BIG BROTHER: Or what if the afterlife is prison? You lie on your cot for eternity. You think about your life. Your family. You regret everything. Every bit of it.

FATHER: Then suck it up twice as hard.

DEAD MOTHER: *Silence.*

LITTLE BROTHER: It will be okay. It's going to be okay.

BIG BROTHER: Or what if you keep living your same life over and over? That's what scares me most. You make the same mistakes again and again. Fuck up in the same ways. Hurt the same people.

FATHER: Why am I here? Why do I have to be here?

DEAD MOTHER: *Silence.*

LITTLE BROTHER: You did some terrible things, but you'll get out someday. You'll have a life. You still have things in front of you. There's still time.

BIG BROTHER: Or what if the prayers change in the sky on the way to God? The words get mangled somehow, so that by the time they get to heaven they mean the opposite of what you intended, or they no longer mean anything at all? And God scratches His head and thinks you are an idiot.

FATHER: Well, you are.

DEAD MOTHER: *Silence.*

LITTLE BROTHER: We love you. We do.

BIG BROTHER: Or what if you die then find out that God is just like Dad? A horse's ass? A true bastard?

FATHER: *Beaming.* Fuck you very much.

DEAD MOTHER: *Silence.*

LITTLE BROTHER: *Silence.*

BIG BROTHER: Wouldn't that be hilarious?

FATHER: I'll beat the crap out of you.

DEAD MOTHER: *Silence.*

LITTLE BROTHER: *Silence.*

BIG BROTHER: You will, Dad. You will.

FATHER: And twice on Sundays.

DEAD MOTHER: *Silence.*

LITTLE BROTHER: *Silence.*

BIG BROTHER: Three times.

FATHER: Okay then.

DEAD MOTHER: *Silence.*

LITTLE BROTHER: *Silence.*

BIG BROTHER: It's settled then.

FATHER: Fair enough. Can we all stop yammering now? Fuck I've got a headache. Anybody hungry?

DEAD MOTHER: *Silence.*

LITTLE BROTHER: *Silence.*

BIG BROTHER: I guess I could eat.

FATHER: Okay then. Okay. Let's have breakfast.

DEAD MOTHER: *Silence.*

LITTLE BROTHER: *Silence.*

The curtain comes down. The curtain is snow or rain. The curtain is a firefly or the flare of a cigarette. The curtain is a prayer battering a ceiling. The curtain is cereal and milk poured in a bowl.

Epilogue

Coyote Moon

My brother claimed he was once a coyote,
which was why he howled at night at passing cars

or even from bar stools, and why he slept by day
in hallways or on grass. But sometimes,

when he was drunk, he reminded me of an evening
snowstorm, the monotone sky alive with commotion,

the frenzy of confetti gathering then trying to suffocate
the land. Once my brother told me how a former

fellow inmate would howl and yip some nights
like a coyote at the moon, and my brother,

unable to resist, would join in, until the guards
came rushing toward them. But the only actual

coyote I ever saw close up was two months after
my brother died, when I emerged from the house

one pre-dawn morning with the trash and saw one
coming up the driveway in falling snow. He didn't make

a sound, but he did pause for a moment
before slipping away into the trees.

Breath

Two years after my brother died,
I received a letter with a return address
from the prison where he spent his final years.
The letter mentioned a book he was reading,
The Maine Woods, which described a place
he'd never been and suspected he would never go,
or even want to, though he admitted
that the length of the sentences had given him
a kind of patience for description
he doubted he would have cultivated
on the outside. There was also a paragraph
that meditated on eating breakfast at 4:30
in the morning, which was what the prison
required of his wing due to overcrowding.
This, too, seemed to him a matter of only
the most mild interest, as though he were floating
through the years on a raft in which
he didn't actually believe. The letter ended
with his attempt at describing a river he could
see from the exercise yard, and how the mist
above that river on cold mornings made him think
of the breath of the long dead, which was not
the kind of idea I ever would have imagined
my brother might have had, especially when combined
with the line from Thoreau with which he brought
the letter to a close: "the spruce and cedar on its shores,
hung with gray lichens, looked at a distance
like the ghosts of trees." That evening I carried
his letter with me past the backyard and to the creek
behind our house, where a faint fog of a night sky
seemed a held breath or maybe a kind of mild fever
that dreams itself into a formalin of memory.
And it occurred to me that the years are torsional,
always twisting in more than one direction at a time,
and this was what the dead would say
if only they could write to us.

Winter Auguries

I think these clouds are drowning
in moonlight.

And the years tuck themselves into the body.

Someone made a prophecy
of frozen snow. I walk across that carapace,
imagining that a dream is an icicle

dangling from a limb, a melting
river of lamentation.

What is there to say about decades
that impale us?

The tongue is a cadence, after all, is thick
in the mouth.

I used to sit with my brother as he drank,

as his words became antlers
or dark blood or unwilling gardens of recriminations.

It must be a comfort to chomp down forever
on that same bitter acorn.

For maybe a clenched fist is supposed to be
an approximation of a heart.

And maybe a clenched heart is supposed to be
an approximation of a fist.

For I believed when we sat at the kitchen table
and watched the winter wind pressing through

the willow's dreadlocks

that a voice could become a kind of dark and perfect
gathering. And snow,

in winter, was parasitic, falling
both in the world and in my brother's chest.

About the Author

Doug Ramspeck is the author of six previous poetry collections and one collection of short stories. His most recent book, *Black Flowers* (2018), was published by LSU Press. Four of his books have received awards: *The Owl That Carries Us Away* (G. S. Sharat Chandra Prize for Short Fiction), *Original Bodies* (Michael Waters Poetry Prize), *Mechanical Fireflies* (Barrow Street Press Poetry Prize), and *Black Tupelo Country* (John Ciardi Prize for Poetry). Individual poems have appeared in journals that include *The Southern Review*, *The Kenyon Review*, *Slate*, and *The Georgia Review*. He is a three-time recipient of an Ohio Arts Council Individual Excellence Award and teaches English at The Ohio State University at Lima.

www.ingramcontent.com/pod-product-compliance
Lightning Source LLC
Chambersburg PA
CBHW071026080526
44587CB00015B/2525